NOTE TO PARENTS:

The Sesame Street Cookbook should be a welcome addition to any child's library. I think you will find the book a marvelously entertaining tool for introducing your child to the wide range of tastes, smells, and textures that good food has to offer. This is important, since most food preferences are developed during the early, formative years.

In selecting recipes for this cookbook, an effort was made to choose ones which would be fun and simple for small children to prepare, with familiar and easily obtainable ingredients. No single recipe is intended to provide a full, well-balanced meal. It's up to you to select recipes and modify ingredients to suit your family budget, schedule, and overall diet.

To get the most nutritive value for the amount of calories your family consumes and for the amount of money you spend on groceries, concentrate on balance, variety, and purity of foods. That means not emphasizing sweets, including many different kinds of food in your diet, and selecting foods as close as possible to the way nature produces them.

You can help establish sound eating habits for your children. Many nutritionists and other health professionals are concerned about the amount of fat, sugar, and unnecessary "additives" that Americans consume and equate with good taste. With your example, encouragement, and enthusiasm, however, your children can develop a genuine appreciation for the more nutritious foods. I think The Sesame Street Cookbook can help.

Angela Raponi-Usobiaga
Angela Raponi-Usobiaga
Public Health Nutritionist

DESIGN BY SALLIE BALDWIN/FRANK SCULLY; BOB ANTLER & SALLIE BALDWIN, INC.

Featuring Jim Henson's Muppets

THE SESAME STREET COOKBOOK

by Pat Tornborg

illustrations by Robert Dennis

Platt & Munk, Publishers/New York
A Division of Grosset & Dunlap

Published by Platt & Munk in conjunction with the Children's Television Workshop

1979 Printing

© 1978 Children's Television Workshop. Muppet characters © 1971, 1972, 1973, 1974, 1976, 1978 Muppets, Inc. Sesame Street ® and the Sesame Street sign are trademarks and service marks of the Children's Television Workshop. All rights reserved. Printed in the United States of America. LIBRARY of CONGRESS CATALOG CARD NUPPET: 77-94382.
ISBN 0-448-47637-1 (TRADE EDITION); ISBN 0-448-13035-1 (LIBRARY EDITION).

CONTENTS

Cooking Words 7
Getting It Together 8
A La Peanut Butter Soup! 9
Little Quiches 11
Tossed Salad 11
Sweet Kisses 11
Oscar's Sardine Specialties 12
Tele-grahams 13
Delicious Dishes 15
Strawberry Mousse 17
The Count's Twenty-Is-Plenty Log 18
Un-cookies 19
Grover's Flights of Fancy 20
Oscar's Junk Food Pie 23
Prairie Dawn's Popcorn Pudding 24
Rubber Duckie Floats 25
Snuffle's Truffles 27
Mrs. Wiggins' Alpha Betty 28
Monster Melon 29
Shake It Awake 31
Bert's Best Breakfasts 32
Secret Dreams 34
Big Bird's Sesame Treats 35
It's Very Easy Bean Green 36
Herry Monster's Mood Food 37
Snuffle-loaf in a Spaghetti Nest 39
Sherlock Hemlock's "P" Soup 41
Twiddle-burgers with Topping 42
Count Your Dressings 43
Big Bird's Best Nests 44
Little Bird's Nest Fillings 45

GOODNESS, LOOK AT ALL THESE CUTE WORDS. I DO NOT KNOW WHAT THEY MEAN, BUT I AM SURE THAT I WILL BY THE TIME I HAVE FINISHED THIS ADORABLE BOOK!

COOKING WORDS

Bake: to cook in the oven.

Beat: to stir ingredients very fast in a bowl, using a spoon or eggbeater. Another word for this is "whip."

Dash: a little bit—as much as would come out of a pepper shaker with one good shake.

*****Dice:** to cut or chop into tiny squares with a knife.

Flake: to make foods like fish into smaller pieces by gently pulling them apart with a fork.

Grate: to make foods like cheese into small crumb-like bits by rubbing them against a rough tool called a "grater."

Grease a pan: to cover all inner surfaces with a light coat of shortening, margarine, or oil.

Ingredient: anything that goes into a recipe.

Knead: to fold, pinch, and squeeze with the hands, as in mixing dough.

*****Mince:** to cut or chop into bits as small as possible with a knife.

Pinch: a tiny bit—as much as you can hold between your thumb and forefinger.

*****Ask a grown-up to help you do this.**

Recipe: a list of edible things, with directions telling how to put them together to make a certain food.

Scald: to heat liquid like milk until tiny bubbles first appear, without letting it boil.

Separate an egg: to take the egg yolk out of the egg white, so that the yolk and white can be used at different times. To separate an egg, break the shell in the middle and hold the two halves of the shell close, so that the white pours out into a bowl and the yolk stays in the shell.

Simmer: to heat liquid until it bubbles gently but doesn't boil, and keep it that way for a while.

*****Slice:** to cut into thin, flat pieces with a sharp knife.

Stir: to mix ingredients in a bowl with a spoon, using a slow, circular motion.

*****Unmold:** to take out of a mold. To unmold, dip the mold into warm water for 10 seconds, being careful not to get the food wet. Put a wet plate over the open top of the mold. Hold the plate and mold together tightly. Flip them over quickly, so that the plate is under the mold. Shake the mold gently, and raise it slowly. If it does not come off easily, apply a hot cloth to the mold until the food slips out.

GETTING IT ALL TOGETHER

"HI, EVERYBODY! IT'S YOUR OLD FRIEND ROOSEVELT FRANKLIN HERE. TODAY WE'RE GOING TO TALK ABOUT DOING THINGS IN THE KITCHEN. DO YOU KNOW ALL THE THINGS I CAN DO IN THE KITCHEN *BY MYSELF?* I CAN..."

- gather the things we need for cooking
- measure amounts
- put things together in a bowl
- mix things with a spoon
- mix things with my hands
- cut things with my own special scissors
- roll things flat with a rolling pin
- crush things to make crumbs
- beat things with an eggbeater
- spread things like fillings and frostings
- grease cookie sheets and baking dishes
- mash things with a fork or spoon
- shake things—but good
- squeeze fruits to get the juice out
- taste things

"SOME THINGS ARE TOO HARD FOR ME, SO *MY MAMA DOES THEM* WHILE I WATCH. SHE MUST..."

- cut with a sharp knife
- slice
- chop
- peel
- heat the oven, and turn on the burners
- open cans

"AND THERE ARE OTHER THINGS THAT MAMA AND I CAN *DO TOGETHER.* WE CAN..."

- put things in the oven to cook
- watch the time things take to cook
- stir things while they're cooking on top of the stove
- pop corn
- clean up
- EAT!

"HEY, DID YOU NOTICE THAT THE LIST OF THINGS *I* CAN DO IS PRETTY LONG?"

"MAMA'S LIST IS MUCH SMALLER. I WONDER HOW SHE EVER GOT ALONG WITHOUT ME!"

A LA PEANUT BUTTER SOUP!

A La Peanut Butter Soup!

To serve four—
What you need:
1 cup of milk
1 can, or 1½ cups of chicken broth
3 tablespoons of chunky peanut butter
½ teaspoon of onion flakes
¼ teaspoon each of salt and paprika

What you do:
Put some water in the bottom half of a double boiler, and put all your ingredients in the top half (not the top hat). Put the double boiler over medium heat. Stir the soup until the peanut butter melts and everything is blended together. The peanut chunks will float on top. When the soup comes to a boil, turn the heat very low and simmer it for 10 minutes.

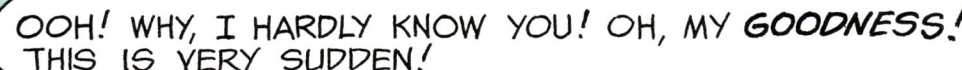

Little Quiches

To serve six—

What you need:

1 tube of refrigerator biscuit rounds (or any uncooked, chilled biscuits)
2 eggs
¾ cup of milk
½ tablespoon of ketchup
¼ teaspoon of salt
½ cup of diced cooked ham (or chicken or fish)
1 tablespoon of minced onion
2 tablespoons of butter
3 tablespoons of grated parmesan cheese

What you do:

While the biscuit dough is still cold and hard, slice 3 biscuits so that you have 6 halves. Put the rest of the dough back in the freezer. Get out 6 aluminum tart pans. (They are sold in supermarkets and dime stores.) Press each biscuit half into a pan so that it covers the bottom and sides of the pan like a pie crust. With a fork, poke tiny holes in the crusts. Bake the crusts in the oven at 375° for 10 minutes, or until they are light brown.

Meanwhile, make the custard filling. Beat the 2 eggs lightly, and stir in the milk, ketchup, and salt. In a pan on top of the stove, cook the minced onion in butter just until it turns brown. Stir in the diced ham, and cook for about 1 minute. Next, mix the ham and onions into the milk and egg mixture.

When the mixture is ready, spoon a little into each crust (about 4 tablespoons apiece). Sprinkle ½ tablespoon of grated cheese onto each quiche. Then line up the little pans on a cookie sheet. Bake them in the oven at 375° for 20 minutes, or until the custard is firm.

Tossed Salad

To serve six—

What you need:

1 head of dark, leafy lettuce (washed and dried)
2 green onions (washed)
½ of a green pepper, with the seeds washed out
12 whole cherry tomatoes (washed)

What you do:

Tear the lettuce into bite-sized pieces with your hands. Put the lettuce in a big salad bowl. Cut the green onions and green pepper with your scissors, making the pieces as small as you can. Add them to the bowl. Then add the whole cherry tomatoes.

Just before you're ready to eat, pour on 2 tablespoons of Just Plain Salad Dressing (see page 43). With a salad fork and spoon, gently toss the salad until all the pieces are coated with dressing. (Don't do it Grover's way.)

Sweet Kisses

To make twelve—

What you need:

1 egg white, separated from the yolk
¾ cup of sugar
½ teaspoon of vanilla
½ cup of chocolate bits

What you do:

Beat the egg white with an eggbeater until it's just stiff enough to stand up in little peaks. Add the sugar, a little at a time, and keep beating until the egg white is very stiff and shiny. Stir in the vanilla, and then the chocolate bits. Drop the batter onto a greased cookie sheet, 1 teaspoon at a time, about 1 inch apart. Bake the kisses in the oven at 300° for 15 minutes, or until they are crisp. (Watch out, Grover!)

OSCAR'S SARDINE SPECIALTIES

YOU KNOW WHY I LIKE SARDINES SO MUCH? 'CAUSE SARDINES ARE LIKE GROUCHES. THEY COME IN A CAN AND HAVE A BAD REPUTATION! HEH! HEH! AND THERE'S ANOTHER WAY SARDINES AND GROUCHES ARE ALIKE. THE SAME KINDS OF THINGS BRING OUT THE **WORST** IN US. THINGS LIKE PICKLES AND ONIONS AND LEMONS. SEE FOR YOURSELF. I'M GOING FISHING.

Sardine and Orange Salad

To serve two—

What you need:
1 can of boneless sardines, drained
2 medium-sized, seedless oranges, peeled
1 purple onion, peeled
6 large, whole lettuce leaves

What you do:
Spread the lettuce leaves on 2 salad plates. Slice each orange across (not down) into 8 slices. Slice the onion across into 14 rings. Put half the sardines in the center of the lettuce on one plate, and half in the center of the lettuce on the other plate. Arrange the orange slices and onion rings in a circle around the sardines on each plate. Put a little Just Plain Salad Dressing (see page 43) on the salad, or eat it just plain.

Sardines in Cucumber Canoes

To serve two—

What you need:
1 medium-sized cucumber, peeled
1 can of boneless sardines, drained
1 hard-boiled egg, chopped fine
1 tablespoon of mayonnaise
1 tablespoon of lemon juice
1 green onion, cut up

What you do:
Slice the peeled cucumber in half lengthwise. Scoop out the seeds so that the cucumber looks like 2 little canoes. Slice a small piece off the bottom of each canoe so that it will sit flat on the plate.

Flake the sardines into a bowl with a fork, and stir in the mayonnaise. Add the lemon juice, onion, and chopped egg, and mix it well. Then spoon half the mixture into each canoe.

Sardine and Pickle on Pumpernickel

To serve two—

What you need:
1 can of boneless sardines, drained
6 chunks of watermelon pickle
4 slices of pumpernickel bread
butter

What you do:
Spread butter on 2 slices of bread. Put half the sardines on each buttered slice of bread. Cut the watermelon pickle into slices about ¼ inch thick, and put some on top of the sardines. Put on the top slices of bread, and you will have Oscar's favorite snack.

PSST! IF YOU THINK SARDINES ARE YUCCHY, USE TUNA FISH IN THESE RECIPES INSTEAD.

DELICIOUS DISHES

"HELLO, COOKIE MONSTER. IT IS I, LOVABLE FURRY OLD GROVER. CAN YOU COME OVER TO MY HOUSE? I HAVE MADE SOME DELICIOUS NEW DISHES, AND..."

"ME BE RIGHT OVER!"

"OH, I AM SO GLAD MY FRIEND COOKIE MONSTER IS COMING TO TASTE MY WONDERFUL TUNA-APPLE SALAD. I WISH I HAD SOME NICE PLATES TO SERVE IT ON. OH, WELL, HE PROBABLY WILL NOT NOTICE."

"YUM, YUM."

The Dishes

To serve two—

What you need:
2 large, firm tomatoes
2 large green peppers
2 celery stalks with heart ends

What you do:
Slice off the tops of the tomatoes and peppers, about ½ inch from the top. Scoop out the insides carefully with a spoon. (Save them for soup or stew.) Make sure to get all the seeds out without breaking the skin of the vegetables. Then wash and dry the celery stalks. Cut off the rough parts of the heart ends. The stalks should be 7 inches long—soup-spoon size.

Tuna-Apple Salad
(for tomato bowls)

To serve two—

What you need:
1 6½-ounce can of tuna, drained
1 large apple, diced
diced ends (about 1 inch) of each celery "spoon"
3 tablespoons of mayonnaise

What you do:
With a fork, flake the tuna into a bowl, and stir in the apple and celery pieces. Add the mayonnaise. Stir everything together. Stuff the salad into the tomato bowls with a real spoon, but eat it with your celery spoon. Then eat your spoon!

Beef-Tomato Juice
(for pepper cups)

To serve two—

What you need:
½ cup of tomato juice, chilled
½ cup of beef broth, chilled
1 teaspoon of lemon juice

What you do:
Stir the 3 ingredients together in a pitcher or large measuring cup, and pour the juice into 2 pepper cups. Drink it up, and then eat your pepper cup. Did you remember to eat your salad bowl? Good! No dishes to wash.

Strawberry Mousse

To serve six—

What you need:
1 egg white, separated from the yolk
¾ cup of heavy cream
1 cup of strawberry jelly
¼ teaspoon of salt

What you do:
Beat the egg white until it's stiff enough to stand up in little peaks. Wash and dry an eggbeater carefully, because next you are going to whip the cream, and the cream won't whip unless the eggbeater is completely dry. Whip the cream until it is nice and fluffy. Stir in the salt. Then wash and dry the eggbeater again. Beat the jelly until all the lumps are out, and stir the smooth jelly into the cream. Stir the egg whites gently into the jelly-cream mixture. Pour the whole thing into a mold or bowl, and freeze it until it's firm—for about 3 hours. Then unmold the mousse.

P.S. If you want to cut down on both the beating and the sweetness of this mousse, replace the jelly with 1 cup of mashed berries, sugared to taste.

GREETINGS! I AM THE COUNT. DO YOU KNOW WHY I AM CALLED THE COUNT? BECAUSE I LOVE TO **COUNT**—ANYTHING! MY VERY FAVORITE RECIPE IS THIS LUNCHTIME LOG THAT IS MADE UP OF TWENTY SEPARATE LITTLE PIECES, AND I COUNT **EACH ONE** AS I MAKE IT!

1, 2, 3. THAT'S ENOUGH FOR ME.
4, 5, 6. HOW MANY SHALL I FIX?
7, 8, 9. I'LL INVITE MY UNCLE AND COUSIN.
ADD 10, 11, AND 12 — AND THAT'S AN EVEN DOZEN.

13, 14, AND 15, IN CASE THERE'S AN EXTRA GUEST.
16, 17, 18 WILL SURELY FEED THE REST.
BUT I WANT TO GO ON COUNTING, SO I'LL ADD 19 AND 20.
I DON'T KNOW **HOW** MANY I'LL FEED, BUT I'LL COUNT ON HAVING **PLENTY!**

THE COUNT'S TWENTY-IS-PLENTY LOG

To serve four or five—
What you need:
1 loaf of snack-sized dark pumpernickel bread
2 3-ounce packages of cream cheese
⅓ cup of orange juice
⅓ cup of chopped nuts (any kind)

What you do:
Let the cream cheese soften before starting. Put the soft cream cheese in a bowl, and pour in the orange juice. Mix them with a wooden spoon until they are as creamy as mayonnaise. Then stir in the chopped nuts.

Count 20 slices of bread, and spread them with cheese. Then make little stacks of bread and cheese. Say the Count's poem as you work. When you've finished stacking, tip each stack onto its side, and push all the stacks end to end. They should stick together like a long log. Frost the log with what's left of the cheese, and put it in the freezer for an hour. Slice the log diagonally.

UN-COOKIES

ME CALLED COOKIE MONSTER BECAUSE ME **LOVE COOKIES!** BUT YOU KNOW WHY COOKIES CALLED "COOKIES?" BECAUSE YOU **COOK** THEM. THEN WHAT WE CALL THESE DELICIOUS COOKIES THAT NOT NEED COOKING? I GUESS THEY "UN-COOKIES," NO?

DO THAT MAKE ME **UN-COOKIE MONSTER?**

To make twenty-four—
What you need:
2 cups of cornflake crumbs
¾ cup of mincemeat (from a box, not a jar)
½ cup of your favorite kind of chopped nuts
2 tablespoons of honey
1 tablespoon of softened butter or margarine
2 tablespoons of lemon juice
confectioners' sugar

What you do:
Put first 3 ingredients in bowl, and mix up good with clean hands. Then put next 3 ingredients in bowl. Keep mixing with hands. (Hands not so clean, now!) Knead until everything all blended.

With both hands, roll batter into little balls, size of 1 tablespoon each. Then roll little balls in sugar. Now you got about 24 yummy Un-cookies and 2 messy hands. Wash messy, sticky hands.

GROVER'S FLIGHTS OF FANCY

The sky sometimes seems like a big bowl of fruit
That is waiting for me. Oh, it all looks so cute!
The moon is a grapefruit, a juicy delight.
The sun is an orange; I'm taking a bite.

I dream that my plane is a big silver spoon,
And I'm eating a chunk of that beautiful moon.
The whole thing is gone after three or four trips,
And the people shout, "There's a total eclipse!"

Then I sprinkle a planet with handfuls of stars,
And I circle around for a nibble of Mars!
When I come back to earth from this wonderful flight,
I have a headful of dreams, and a big appetite!

Sun Jelly Sundae
To serve four—
What you need:
1 envelope of unflavored gelatin
¾ cup of cold water
1 can of frozen orange juice concentrate, just thawed
½ cup of very cold water
3 mandarin orange sections
Juicifruit Dressing (see page 43)

What you do:
Pour ¾ cup of cold water into a saucepan, and sprinkle in the gelatin. Stir it over low heat for 3 minutes, just until it melts. Turn off the heat, and let the gelatin cool for about 5 minutes. Pour in the orange juice concentrate. Stir in the ½ cup of very cold water. Then pour it all into a mold or round-bottomed bowl. Put it in the refrigerator.

After about half an hour, when the gel is partly set, push the orange sections all the way down to the bottom of the bowl. That way they will come out on top when the gelatin is unmolded. Leave the mold in the refrigerator until you are ready to serve it, or for at least another hour. Unmold the Sun Jelly. Serve it with a pitcher of Juicifruit Dressing on the side (see page 43).

Full-Moon Salads

Follow the Sun Jelly recipe, but use frozen grapefruit juice concentrate instead of orange juice, and pieces of pineapple ring instead of orange sections. Mold the gel in 4 small, round-bottomed bowls so that each person has a full moon.

When the gel is partly set, press the pieces of pineapple ring to the bottom to make the eyes and mouth. Unmold the moons onto 4 salad plates spread with lettuce. If you like, put several chunks of avocado on each plate. This salad is good with Just Plain Salad Dressing (see page 43).

OSCAR'S JUNK FOOD PIE

Oscar's Junk Food Pie

To serve four or five—

What you need:
¾ cup of cornflake crumbs
1 tablespoon of sugar
2 tablespoons of soft margarine or butter
2 eggs, separated
1 12-ounce can of sweetened, condensed milk
⅓ cup of fresh lemon juice
2 tablespoons of sugar

What you do:
With your fingers, mix the crumbs, 1 tablespoon of sugar, and the soft margarine or butter in an ice tray or glass pie plate. Spoon out 2 tablespoons of crumbs, and set them aside for topping. Press the rest of the crumbs evenly and firmly around the sides and bottom of the ice tray to make a nice crust.

Beat the egg yolks with an eggbeater until they are bright lemon-yellow (for about 1 minute). Stir in the condensed milk and lemon juice.

Next, wash and dry the eggbeater, and beat the egg whites until they are stiff enough to stand in little peaks. Sprinkle in 2 tablespoons of sugar, one at a time, and beat the whites a bit each time you do this.

Stir the egg whites into the yolk mixture very gently, until the mixture becomes a pale yellow. Pour the filling into the crust. Sprinkle the crumbs you saved on top, and freeze the pie until it's firm (for about 2 hours).

> HEY, PARDNERS, I'LL BET YOU NEVER THOUGHT OF POPCORN AS A **REAL FOOD**, JUST BECAUSE IT'S SUCH A GOOD SNACK! BUT IT'S REALLY A CEREAL, LIKE WHEAT OR RICE. THE PILGRIMS ATE HOT BUTTERED POPCORN WITH MILK ON IT FOR BREAKFAST. YOU CAN, TOO! OR HAVE IT COLD WITH YOUR FAVORITE FRUIT AND MILK. HOT BUTTERED POPCORN SPRINKLED WITH PARMESAN CHEESE IS YUMMY IN ANY KIND OF SOUP, INSTEAD OF CROUTONS OR CRACKERS. AND BUTTERED POPCORN SPRINKLED WITH GARLIC SALT MAKES GOOD CRUNCHIES IN A TOSSED SALAD!

PRAIRIE DAWN'S POPCORN PUDDING

Prairie Dawn's Popcorn Pudding

To serve six—
What you need:
2½ quarts of popped corn
4 cups of milk, scalded
1 egg, lightly beaten with a fork
¾ cup of sugar
¾ cup of raisins
½ teaspoon each of nutmeg, cinnamon, and allspice

> ♪ HOME, HOME ON THE RANGE... ♫

What to do:
Crush the popcorn into fine crumbs with a rolling pin. Put the crumbs and the milk in a bowl. Cover the bowl with a plate, and let the mixture soak for about 2 hours at room temperature.

Stir in all the other ingredients. Mix them well. Then pour the mixture into a greased baking dish. Bake the pudding for 1 hour at 300°. Serve it hot with vanilla ice cream or cold applesauce.

Oh, I love to take a bath
When I'm feeling kind of grubby.
I just grab my Rubber Duckie,
And I hop into the tubby.

But bathing does remind me
Of another kind of treat.
The bubbles make me hungry;
They look good enough to eat.

RUBBER DUCKIE FLOATS

The water makes me thirsty,
And my Duckie makes me think
Of a cool and frothy soda
That is both a food and drink.

So I'll fix a Rubber Duckie Float.
That's sure to quench my thirst
As it gurgles down my little throat!
But I'll finish washing first.

Rubber Duckie Floats

To serve two—
What you need:
1 pint of lemon sherbet
½ cup of crushed pineapple, drained (save the juice)
1 tablespoon of pineapple juice from the can
1 small bottle of ginger ale
2 whole pineapple rings

What you do:
Put 2 scoops of sherbet, the crushed pineapple, and 1 tablespoon of pineapple juice in a bowl. Mix them with an eggbeater. Pour the mixture into 2 tall soda glasses, and put 1 whole scoop of sherbet in each glass. Pour the ginger ale slowly into the glasses until the sodas become sudsy. Don't let the suds overflow. Hang a pineapple ring on each glass, and serve the floats with a straw and a spoon.

Snuffle's Truffles

To make twelve—

What you need:

1 8-ounce package of cream cheese, softened
1 tablespoon of honey
⅓ cup of raisins, cut small
2 tablespoons of chopped nuts (any kind you like)
12 chocolate wafers, crushed with a rolling pin

What you do:

While the cream cheese is getting soft at room temperature, cut the raisins into small bits with your scissors. But before you do, put a little

salad oil on the blades of the scissors so the raisins won't stick to them.

Next, stir the cream cheese, honey, raisins, and nuts together with a wooden spoon until they are well mixed. Roll the mixture into bite-sized balls with clean hands. Then roll the balls in the chocolate wafer crumbs. If these treats aren't eaten up right away, keep what's left over in the refrigerator.

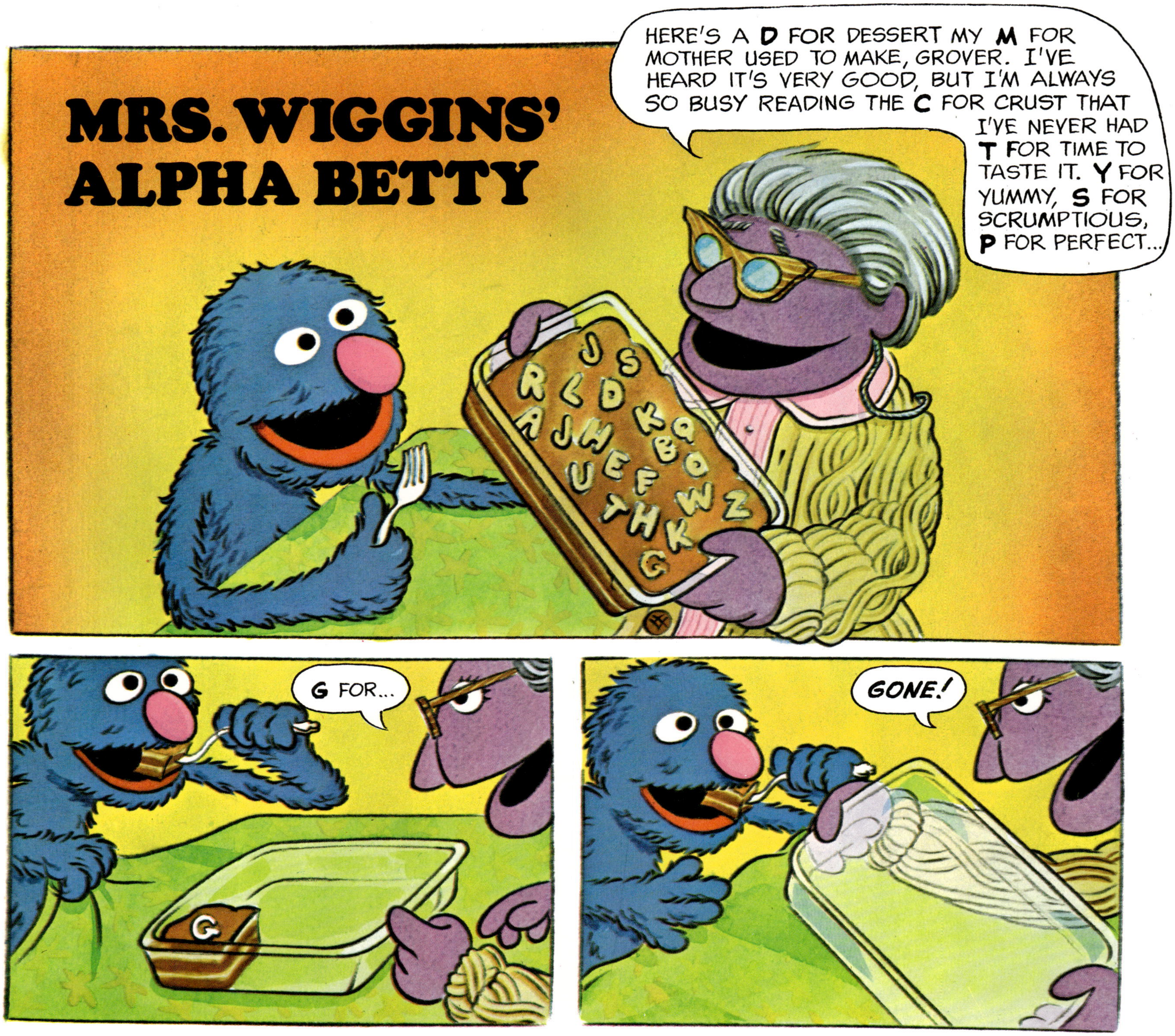

MRS. WIGGINS' ALPHA BETTY

Mrs. Wiggins' Alpha Betty

To serve six—

What you need:
1 12-ounce jar (1½ cups) of unsweetened applesauce
1 cup of graham cracker or zwieback crumbs
3 tablespoons of butter
1 cup of alphabet breakfast cereal

What you do:
Crush enough graham crackers or zwiebacks to make 1 cup of crumbs. Melt the butter in a frying pan and put the crumbs in it, stirring them quickly until they turn brown. Choose a shallow baking dish or glass pie dish, and sprinkle in a thin layer of crumbs. Spread on a thin layer of applesauce. Then add another layer of crumbs and another layer of applesauce, until you have used all the crumbs and applesauce. Make sure your last layer is applesauce. Cover it with alphabet letters. Bake it in the oven at 375° for 30 minutes. Then pour either light cream or softened vanilla ice cream over the alphabet letters, and serve the Alpha Betty right away.

MONSTER MELON

Step 1:
Take 1 huge watermelon, and have a grown-up slice off the top quarter the long way. Have a little piece sliced off the bottom, too. Then the watermelon won't roll away. With a big spoon, take the watermelon out of the rind. Throw away the seeds. Then cut the melon into bite-sized chunks, and put all the chunks back into the melon rind.

Step 2:
Slice 3 or 4 bananas into flat, round pieces, and toss them in with the melon chunks.

Step 3:
Next, throw in 3 cups of seedless grapes, and mix it all with your big spoon.

Step 4:
Put scoops of orange, pineapple, and lime sherbet on top.

Step 5:
Sprinkle on some chopped nuts. Then pour on some Juicifruit Dressing (see page 43).

LITTLE JERRY AND THE MONOTONES

SHAKE IT AWAKE

> You don't wanna get up,
> You don't wanna get dressed,
> And that noisy old rooster's
> Just being a pest.
>
> And you wish your alarm clock
> Would jump in the lake.
> There's just one thing to do,
> And that's SHAKE IT AWAKE!
>
> You don't wanna fry eggs,
> You don't wanna cook bacon.
> You don't want whatever
> Big brother is makin.'
>
> You don't want ice cream
> Or a three-layer cake.
> There's just one thing to do,
> And that's MAKE IT A SHAKE!

"THAT WOKE UP THE WHOLE TOWN!"

"YES, THAT WAS ALARMING!"

Shake It Awake

To serve two—

What you need:
1 8-ounce glass of milk
1 whole egg
1 8-ounce glass of orange juice
2 orange slices

What you do:
Put everything but the orange slices into a bowl or pitcher. Mix the ingredients with an eggbeater until frothy. Pour the shakes into 2 glasses, hang an orange slice on each glass (like a rising sun), and sit down to breakfast.

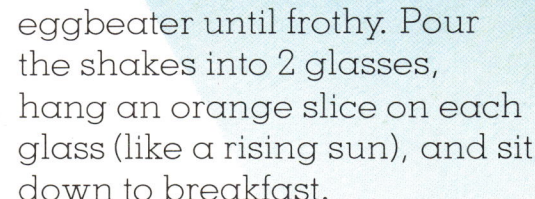

BERT'S BEST BREAKFASTS

Oatmeal Burgers

To serve one—
What you need:
leftover cooked oatmeal
bread crumbs
½ tablespoon of butter

What you do:
Take a bowl of leftover cooked oatmeal out of the refrigerator. With a large, round spoon, dish out patties about 2 inches wide and about ½ inch thick. Then, with clean hands, put them on a plate covered with bread crumbs. Turn them over once, so that both sides are covered with crumbs. Next, for each oatmeal burger, put ½ tablespoon of butter in a frying pan. Fry the oatmeal burgers until they are dark brown and crispy on both sides. Then put them in a bowl and pour some milk on them, or put a little spoonful of apple butter on each one.

Oatmeal Soup

To serve two—
What you need:
⅓ cup of old-fashioned oats
1½ cups of water
½ cup of milk
¼ teaspoon of salt
¼ cup of raisins

What you do:
Pour the water and milk into a pan on top of the stove, and bring them to a boil. Then stir in the raisins, oats, and salt. Turn down the heat, and let the mixture bubble gently for about 7 minutes. Stir it 3 or 4 times while it's cooking. When it's ready, just pour and eat.

SECRET DREAMS

Secret Dreams

What you need:
1 package of pecan halves
1 box of pitted dates
confectioners' sugar

What you do:
Open the dates and hide a pecan half inside each one. Then roll each date in a dish of confectioners' sugar until it's lightly coated. Don't tell your friends what's inside. Let them find out the secret themselves.

Sesame Treats

What you need:
1 cup of toasted sesame seeds (If you can't buy them toasted, toast them in the oven at 250° for about 10 minutes, until golden.)
⅔ cup of honey

What you do:
Cook the honey in a heavy-bottomed pot until the candy thermometer reads 265°. (Watch the thermometer carefully, because the temperature must be exact.) Then stir in the seeds and mix them well. Take the pot off the stove. Grease a cookie pan, and pour in the honey-seed mixture, spreading it evenly in a layer about ¼ inch thick. It will harden as it cools. Then you can break it into bite-sized Sesame Treats!

MOOD FOOD

Mood Food

What you need:

For the face: lettuce; red cabbage; slices of cheese or meat

For the eyes: hard-boiled eggs, sliced lengthwise or across; sliced green or black olives

For the mouth: slices of melon or half of a banana, curved upward or downward; a pineapple ring (for a surprised mouth); a strawberry cut in half

For the ears: a pear cut in quarters lengthwise

For the nose and cheeks: cherries, berries, or cherry tomatoes, cut in half

For the hair: shredded carrots, cole slaw, bean or alfalfa sprouts

What you do:
Just place the ingredients of your choice together to make a face that shows your mood.

SNUFFLE-LOAF IN A SPAGHETTI NEST

"OH, DEAR. THAT'S REALLY BEAUTIFUL, BIRD. THANK YOU."

Snuffle-loaf in a Spaghetti Nest

To serve four or five—

What you need:
1 pound of chopped meat
1 whole egg
¾ cup of bread crumbs
2 tablespoons of milk
2 tablespoons of onion flakes
2 teaspoons of salt
½ teaspoon of dry mustard
1 small piece of hard-boiled egg white
1 black olive

What you do:
Put all the ingredients except the hard-boiled egg white and the black olive into a big bowl. Mix them with clean hands until they are blended together. Then shape the mixture with your hands to look like the picture. Keep Snuffie's tail and trunk curled close to his body so they don't overcook. Bake the loaf in the oven at 400° for 50 minutes.

When the loaf is cooked, with your scissors cut little pieces of the egg white and the olive to make eyes. Fasten the olive and egg white pieces together with half the length of a toothpick stuck in from behind. To hold the eyes in place, put the end of the toothpick which is sticking out into the cooked loaf. Remember not to let anyone eat the toothpick.

To make the spaghetti nest, cook an 8-ounce package of spaghetti just the way the box tells you to. Drain the water, and stir in 3 tablespoons of butter. On a large, round platter, arrange the spaghetti in a ring, leaving a space in the center large enough to hold your Snuffle-loaf. Put the Snuffle-loaf carefully in the nest, and have Snuffle-upagus for dinner!

SHERLOCK HEMLOCK, SOUPER SLEUTH

Sherlock Hemlock, the world's greatest detective, was walking through a big forest one day. All of a sudden, he heard a low growl nearby. He looked high and he looked low, but he saw no bear, no mountain lion, and no stray dog.

Then Sherlock Hemlock heard the growl again! He took out his pocket watch and looked at it. "Egad!" he cried. "It's just as I suspected. Lunchtime. My tummy is growling to tell me it's time to eat."

At that very moment, Sherlock Hemlock saw what he thought was a restaurant through the trees. He ran right over, hoping he could get a table without a reservation. But when he stepped inside, he found the place completely empty.

Sitting on a table, however, were three steaming bowls of soup.

"Hmmm!" exclaimed Sherlock Hemlock. "I, the world's greatest detective, strongly suspect that this is a baffling mystery! This is the only restaurant for miles; it's lunchtime; there's nobody here; and there are three bowls of hot soup on the table. The question is: what kind of soup is it?"

Sherlock Hemlock studied the first bowl of soup. "Hmmm. There are some clues to consider. The soup is green, and it has letters floating in it. In fact, I see the letter 'E.' It might be 'E' soup. But there's no such thing as 'E' soup."

"Maybe the second bowl will give me more clues," he said, moving on to examine it. "Hmmm. This soup is green, too, and it has little letters floating in it. In fact, I see the letter 'C' floating in it. It might be 'C' soup. But there's no such thing as 'C' soup."

The third bowl of soup looked very much like the other two. The case was beginning to look like a tough one to crack, when Sherlock Hemlock, the world's greatest detective, spotted yet another clue. The third bowl had the letter "P" floating in it. "Egad, I've got it!" he cried.

"This letter 'P' must mean that this is 'P' soup! Those little green things are peas! Phew! I'm sure glad the mystery is solved so that I can finally eat it!" And with that he sat down and ate a bowlful of "P" soup.

"P" Soup

To serve three—

What you need:
1½ cups of fresh peas, or 1 package of frozen peas
1 can (or 1 cup) of chicken broth
½ cup of water
⅓ cup of cut green onions
½ teaspoon of salt
¼ teaspoon of pepper
½ cup of heavy cream (or ½ cup of milk enriched with 2 tablespoons of powdered milk)
½ cup of cooked alphabet noodles

What you do:
Put everything but the noodles and the cream in a large pot with a heavy bottom. When the soup boils, turn down the heat and let it simmer gently for about 15 minutes.

Pour the soup through a strainer into another pot so that all the peas are gathered in the strainer. Spoon out ½ cup of the peas and put them aside in a bowl. Then mash the rest of the peas through the strainer with a wooden spoon, stirring them back into the soup. Now put in the whole peas that you set aside, and stir in the cooked alphabet noodles. Reheat the soup, stirring in the cream or milk. Serve the souper sleuth's super soup piping hot.

TWIDDLE RIDDLES

Q: Where do Twiddle-bugs take the kids on Sunday afternoons?
A: To McTwiddle's for Twiddle-burgers!

Q: What do you call a Twiddle-burger that's not too small and not too big?
A: A Middle-twiddle!

Q: What does Mr. McTwiddle cook his Twiddle-burgers on?
A: A Twiddle-griddle!

Q: What do Twiddle-kiddles like best at McTwiddles?
A: Little Twiddle-burgers with Special Twiddle Topping!

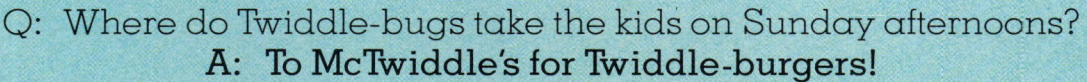

Little Twiddle-burgers
To serve five—
What you need:
1 pound of ground round or chuck beef
⅓ cup of raisins
salt and pepper

What you do:
Sprinkle the raisins into the hamburger meat and twiddle the mixture with your hands until the raisins are well mixed with the meat. Make 5 flat patties, and cook them on both sides in your Twiddle-griddle, or skillet, until nice and brown. Take them out with a spatula. Put each Twiddle-burger on a sesame seed bun and spread on Special Twiddle Topping.

Special Twiddle Topping
To serve five—
What you need:
1 medium-sized zucchini squash, sliced thin
1 big golden delicious apple, quartered and sliced thin
2 tablespoons of butter or margarine
½ teaspoon of celery salt
½ teaspoon of nutmeg

What you do:
Melt the butter or margarine in a skillet, and put in the squash and apple slices. Cover the skillet. Cook the squash and apples for about 7 minutes, or until they're soft, stirring them once in a while. Stir in the seasonings. Now the Special Twiddle Topping is ready to be spread on your Twiddle-burgers.

Q: What do you call boys and girls who love Twiddle-burgers?
A: Twiddle-kiddles!

COUNT YOUR DRESSINGS

"YOU KNOW HOW I LOVE TO COUNT, SO I ALWAYS ASK FOR THE COUNTING JOBS. THIS TIME I'VE COUNTED THE **DRESSINGS** IN THIS BOOK. WHAT ARE DRESSINGS, YOU ASK? A DRESSING IS A LOVELY THING THAT YOU PUT ON SOMETHING ELSE TO MAKE BOTH THINGS EVEN BETTER. LET ME SHOW YOU."

"HERE I AM IN MY SUIT. ONE WONDERFUL COUNT! AND HERE IS MY DRAMATIC CAPE. WATCH WHAT HAPPENS WHEN I PUT IT **ON**."

1. Lemon Cream Mayonnaise

To make one cup—
What you need:
1/3 cup of mayonnaise
1 tablespoon of confectioners' sugar
1 pinch of salt
1 1/2 tablespoons of lemon juice
1/3 cup of heavy cream

What you do:
Whip the cream with an eggbeater until it's stiff and fluffy. Then stir in all the other ingredients until it is smooth.

2. Just Plain Salad Dressing

To make one cup—
What you need:
3/4 cup of salad oil
1/4 cup of vinegar
1 crushed clove of garlic
3/4 teaspoon of salt
1/4 teaspoon of sugar
dash of pepper

What you do:
Put all these ingredients in a jar, and put a tight-fitting lid on it. Shake the jar well. Just before you pour the dressing, shake the jar again.

3. Chinese Salad Dressing

To make one cup—
What you need:
1 cup of Just Plain Salad Dressing
1 tablespoon of soy sauce

What you do:
Add the soy sauce to the Just Plain Salad Dressing, and shake it well. Remember to shake the jar again just before pouring.

4. Juicifruit Dressing

To make two cups—
What you need:
1 package of frozen strawberries in syrup
1 can of crushed pineapple, drained (You can drink the juice)

What you do:
Let the berries thaw. Then stir them in with the pineapple.

BIG BIRD'S BEST NESTS

OF ALL THE THINGS THAT I CAN DO, THERE'S ONE THAT I DO BEST. I'D LIKE TO SHARE THIS THING WITH YOU... IT'S HOW TO BUILD A NEST!

THERE ISN'T ONLY ONE SORT; THERE ARE NESTS OF MANY KINDS, MADE OF CRISPY NOODLES, PRETZEL STICKS, OR EVEN MELON RINDS!

Noodle Nests

To serve two—
Divide the crispy noodles from 1 10-ounce can onto 2 salad plates. With clean fingers, hollow out a little place in the center of each pile of noodles. Be careful not to let your parakeet see the nests. He might move right in!

Pretzel Nests

To serve two—
Since pretzels don't hold together quite as well as crispy noodles, it's best to make these nests in a soup or cereal bowl. Just put in a large handful of pretzel sticks and hollow out a place in the center.

Melon Nests

To serve two—
Cut a medium-sized melon in half, and scoop out the seeds. With a soup spoon, take out most of the melon, leaving the rind and skin about ½ inch thick. Sprinkle the inside of the nest with shredded coconut.

LITTLE BIRD'S NEST FILLINGS

BIG BIRD IS RIGHT, A NEST IS FUN! YOU'LL SEE AS YOU BEGIN IT. BUT I MUST ADD, IT'S BETTER STILL WITH SOMETHING YUMMY IN IT!

Cold Vegetable Salad

To serve two—

What you need:
1 cup of chilled cooked vegetables (Leftovers are perfect.)
2 tablespoons of Chinese Salad Dressing (See page 43.)
1 small can of water chestnuts, whole

What you do:
Put the cold vegetables in a bowl and pour on the salad dressing. Toss the vegetables gently with a fork and spoon, and divide them evenly between the 2 noodle nests. Put 2 whole water chestnuts on top of each salad. They will look like eggs.

Melonberry Salad

To serve two—

What you need:
melon balls scooped from melon halves
1/3 cup of blueberries or strawberries
1/3 cup of seedless green grapes
shredded coconut

What you do:
Sprinkle shredded coconut in the melon nests. Mix all the fruit in a bowl, and spoon it evenly into the two melon nests. Pour some Lemon Cream Mayonnaise (see page 43) over the top.

Egg Salad

To serve two—

What you need:
3 hard-boiled eggs, chopped coarsely
1/4 cup of chopped celery
1/4 cup of mayonnaise
1 teaspoon of mustard
1/2 teaspoon of salt
dash of pepper
black olives

What you do:
Mix the mustard and mayonnaise and salt and pepper. Stir in the celery. Then stir in the chopped eggs. Put half of the egg salad into each nest of pretzel sticks, and put 1 or 2 black olive "eggs" on top.